# Learn to
# MAKE A QUILT
## from start to finish

HOUSE of
WHITE
BIRCHES

PUBLISHERS

# Table of Contents

*These 5 quilts were done by staff members at House of White Birches. All were new or beginner quilters.*

# Introduction

When I first started quilting, I found I made a lot of unnecessary mistakes because everyone that taught me assumed I knew certain things. By their assuming I knew these things, my first, second and third quilting journeys were on bumpy roads. Actually, they were filled with potholes.

As I watched others quilt, I started asking why they did things the way they did them. And as I asked the questions and learned the answers the road got smoother.

This book will address those unasked questions and the answers that are assumed. A new quilter needs information to make a successful attempt at her or his first quilt. We want you to have the knowledge to go on to your next quilt project with the confidence that you can do it.

We want your first quilting experience to be a great one. We have picked a block pattern that will address certain common techniques that a new quilter needs to know. This block also allows for many setting possibilities. You can make it with any style of fabric so long as you have lights and darks for contrast. This quilt can truly be your creation in every way. Pick the fabrics you like. Your choices will dictate if it is traditional, vintage or contemporary.

It's a great first-quilt project, and one you may choose to do again. I sometimes like to look at a photo of my first quilt—I call it my "humility quilt"—to prove how far I have come in my quilting. It also reminds me that I have much more to learn.

In the ever-changing world of quilting, there is always something new and exciting to learn. Your journey has just begun. May all your quilt journeys be successful! ❖

# Meet the Designer

Carolyn S. Vagts is a wife, mother, grandmother, quilt designer and the editor of *Quilter's World*. She also has a successful quilt shop in Canterbury Village in Lake Orion, Mich. Carolyn has made a name for herself in the quilting world with her award-winning techniques of mixing traditional piecing with fusible art appliqué. She especially likes to teach beginning quilting classes, wanting every quilter to have a good first experience with quilting. She also lectures and teaches workshops to guilds.

Carolyn's designs have been published regularly in several magazines, including *Quilter's World*. She has had many designs published in quilting books as well. Many of her exclusive designs can be found at Clotilde.com.

The creative process has been a notable part of her life. She studied drawing, pottery and sculpture in college and received a liberal arts degree. She finally found her niche in quilting when asked to do some design work. That was ten years ago, and she has been designing quilts and working in the quilt industry ever since. ❖

House of White Birches, Berne, Indiana 46711 Clotilde.com

# Beginning Quilting 101

## Project Notes

The Ollie's Square block pattern was selected to help you learn basic quiltmaking skills. This block has large pieces that are stitched together with straight seams. All cutting can be done with a rotary cutter and ruler on a cutting mat.

Specific skills, such as selecting the pattern, choosing fabrics, quiltmaking tools and more are detailed in other sections of this book. It would be helpful for you to read this information before starting this quilt.

For this pattern, select two fabrics with contrast to make the blocks—one light and one dark fabric. One other fabric was introduced in a narrow

inner border that separates the blocks from the outer borders.

The fabrics listed and instructions given result in a long twin-size quilt, which is a nice beginner-size quilt.

If you prefer to make a larger quilt, it is easy to accomplish by adding more borders or wider borders while keeping the number of blocks the same.

More blocks may also be added to enlarge a quilt, but the block layout may need to change, depending on the way you set the blocks together. To change the layout of the blocks, refer to the gallery of quilts at the end of this book and the Alternate Placement Diagrams on pages 43-47 for layout suggestions. ❖

# Twist & Turn Quilt

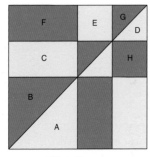

**Ollie's Square**
12" x 12" Block
Make 24

## Project Specifications
- Quilt Size: 54" x 78"
- Finished Block Size: 12" x 12"
- Number of Blocks: 24

## Basic Quilting Tools & Supplies
There are some basic tools and supplies that are not listed with every pattern, but are very important to successful quiltmaking.
- Basic sewing machine—one with a straight stitch is all you will need for this quilt.
- Quilting rulers—these are used for measuring and cutting. A 6½" x 24" ruler and a 6½" square are used in this project. A 12½" square is also helpful.
- 45mm rotary cutter
- 24" x 36", self-healing cutting mat
- Water-soluble fabric markers for light and dark fabrics
- Matching or neutral-color (such as gray or tan) cotton thread for piecing
- Cotton quilting thread
- Quilting/betweens or sharps hand-sewing needles
- Machine needles, Microtex 10/70 are recommended
- Glass head fine straight pins
- Quilter's curved safety pins
- Shears or scissors
- Seam ripper

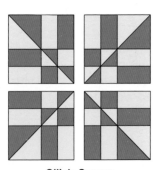

**Ollie's Square**
Alternate arrangement of units
to make a different block

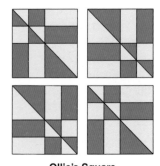

**Ollie's Square**
Alternate arrangement of units
to make a different block

6

## Fabric & Batting

The following is a list of fabrics needed to make the quilt as shown. Measurements are based on 42" usable fabric width. Refer to Pattern & Fabric Selection on page 14 for more information about choosing and preparing fabric.

- 1⅞ yards light fabric for blocks
- 2¼ yards dark fabric for blocks and outer borders
- ½ yard contrasting fabric for inner borders
- ⅝ yard coordinating fabric for binding—should coordinate with fabrics used in the quilt, or can be the same fabric as borders
- Backing 62" x 86" (5 yards 42"-wide fabric)
- Batting 62" x 86" (72" x 90" twin-size packaged batting, trimmed to size)

## Cutting for 24 Blocks

Refer to Cutting Your Fabric Using a Rotary Cutter on page 22 for more specific information about fabric preparation and rotary cutting techniques before beginning to cut.

Block pieces are assigned letters for easy reference. After cutting, stack like pieces together and attach a sticky note with the assigned letter written on it to the top of each pile. Keep all same-size and same-fabric pieces stacked together until selected for piecing

**1.** Straighten fabric and iron; fold fabric in half and straighten ends before cutting.

**2.** Cut two 6⅞" by fabric width strips light fabric (See Cutting Your Fabric Using a Rotary Cutter on page 22 for instructions on cutting strips wider than your ruler); subcut strips into (12) 6⅞" squares. Cut each square in half on one diagonal to make a total of 24 A triangles as shown in Figure 1.

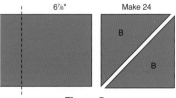

**Figure 1**

**3.** Cut four 6½" by fabric width strips light fabric; subcut strips into (48) 3½" x 6½" C rectangles as shown in Figure 2.

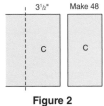

**Figure 2**

**4.** Cut three 3⅞" by fabric width strips light fabric; subcut strips into (24) 3⅞" squares. Cut each square in half on one diagonal to make a total of 48 D triangles as shown in Figure 3.

**Figure 3**

**5.** Cut two 3½" by fabric width strips light fabric; subcut strips into (24) 3½" E squares as shown in Figure 4.

**Figure 4**

**6.** Cut two 6⅞" by fabric width strips dark fabric 1; subcut strips into (12) 6⅞" squares. Cut each square in half on one diagonal to make 24 B triangles as shown in Figure 5.

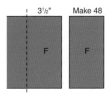

**Figure 5**

**7.** Cut four 6½" by fabric width strips dark fabric 1; subcut strips into (48) 3½" x 6½" F rectangles as shown in Figure 6.

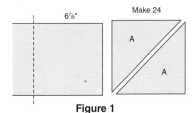

**Figure 6**

**8.** Cut three 3⅞" by fabric width strips dark fabric 1; subcut strips into (24) 3⅞" squares. Cut each square in half on one diagonal to make 48 G triangles as shown in Figure 7.

**Figure 7**

**9.** Cut two 3½" by fabric width strips dark fabric 1; subcut strips into (24) 3½" H squares as shown in Figure 8.

**Figure 8**

**10.** Cut seven 2" by fabric width strips from dark fabric 1 for K and L outer borders.

**11.** Cut seven 1½" by fabric width strips from contrasting fabric 1 for I and J inner borders.

**12.** Cut seven 2½" by fabric width strips from coordinating binding fabric.

## Before You Begin to Sew Your Quilt Top

Quilting has several important things that beginners should know when piecing their quilt tops. We recommend you follow these guidelines for accuracy and best use of your time. Refer to Construction Techniques on page 25 for greater detail about seam allowances, pressing and chain piecing.

### Seam Allowance

Quilters generally use a ¼" seam allowance when piecing, so a ¼" seam allowance is included in the cutting sizes for all quilt pieces. An accurate seam allowance is a must for precise piecing.

### Pressing

After pieces are joined in units, the seams need to be pressed. To begin, press along the stitched seam to set the seam and then open the stitched unit and press seams as stated in the pattern instructions. You will be instructed about the direction to press seams with each step. Pressing without steam is recommended to avoid stretching the pieces out of shape.

### Chain Piecing

Chain piecing is a term used to describe joining a large number of pieces without stopping and starting with individual pieces as shown in Figure 9. This saves time, thread and trips to the ironing board. Always stitch pieces right sides together.

### Piecing the Blocks

Just one block pattern is used in this quilt. The block may be positioned in varying ways in rows to create different patterns. However, the blocks are all pieced in the same way. You will be assembling units for all blocks at the same time. After these units are pieced, they are joined to complete the blocks.

## Stitching the Pieced Units for Blocks

**1.** Select one light C rectangle and one dark F rectangle; place the two pieces with the right sides together, aligning edges.

**2.** Sew a ¼" seam allowance along one 6½" side of the layered C-F pair. Repeat to make 48 C-F units by chain piecing (without cutting the thread) as shown in Figure 9.

**Figure 9**

**3.** Cut the threads between the units to separate units. Set seams by ironing over each seam. Open each unit and press seams toward F, the darker fabric piece, as shown by the arrow in Figure 10. Stack the units together and label C-F.

**Figure 10**

**4.** Select one each light A and dark B triangle; place with right sides together and sew along the long diagonal side as shown in Figure 11. Repeat to make 24 A-B units using the chain-piecing technique.

**Figure 11**

**5.** Separate units, set the seam and press with seams toward B as shown in Figure 12. *Note: The stitched units will now measure 6½" square and will have little triangular "dog ears" at the seam corners as shown in Figure 13.*

**Figure 12**

**Figure 13**

House of White Birches, Berne, Indiana 46711   Clotilde.com

**6.** Trim the dog ears from each A-B unit and stack the units together referring to Figure 14.

**Figure 14**

**7.** Repeat steps 4–6 with the D and G triangles to make a total of 48 D-G units as shown in Figure 15.

Make 48

**Figure 15**

### Completing the Blocks

**1.** Select one D-G unit and one E square; lay these out and join to make a row referring to Figure 16. Set the seam and then press toward the E square.

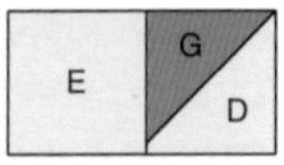

**Figure 16**

**2.** Repeat step 1 with an H square and one D-G unit as shown in Figure 17; set and press the seam toward the H square.

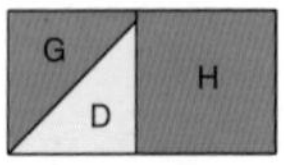

**Figure 17**

**3.** Arrange the two units, nesting seams one against the other; join the two pieced units to make a corner unit as shown in Figure 18. Press seam to one side. ***Note:*** *When seams that have been pressed in opposite directions are joined, the seams nest beside one another, making it easy to make perfectly matched seams when stitching is complete.* Refer to Construction Techniques on page 25.

Make 24

**Figure 18**

**4.** Repeat steps 1–3 to complete a total of 24 corner units. Stack units together and label as corner units.

**5.** To complete one Ollie's Square block, sew a C-F unit to a corner unit to make a row, matching seams as shown in Figure 19. Press seam toward the C-F unit.

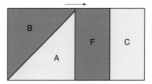

**Figure 19**

**6.** Sew an A-B unit to the F side of a C-F unit to make a second row as shown in Figure 20. Press seam toward the C-F unit.

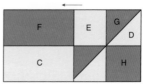

**Figure 20**

**7.** Join the two rows to complete one Ollie's Square block as shown in Figure 21, nesting seams. Press seam toward the second row.

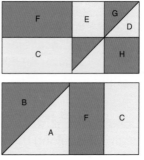

**Figure 21**

**8.** Repeat steps 5–7 to complete a total of 24 Ollie's Square blocks. ***Note:*** *Each block should measure 12½" square at this time if your seam allowances have been a consistent ¼". Refer to Square-Up the Blocks in Construction Techniques on page 25.*

### Completing the Pieced Quilt Top

When the blocks are all pieced and a consistent size, they are ready to be joined. You may lay them out on a bed or floor in six rows of four blocks each. Start rotating the blocks to create a setting order. This traditional block can be set in many different ways to create different designs. The Twist & Turn Placement Diagram on page 9 used for this pattern is a light and dark pinwheel design. Refer to the Putting It All Together section in Construction

Techniques, page 25, the Alternate Placement Diagrams on pages 43–47 and the quilt gallery at the back of this book for other setting variations for the Ollie's Square block.

### Tips & Techniques

• *Taking a digital photo of each setting as it is arranged makes it easy for you to see how all the setting choices look and enables you to make the perfect choice without having to unstitch seams.*

**1.** Arrange the blocks in six rows of four blocks each referring to Figure 22.

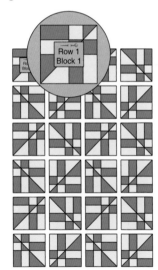

**Figure 22**

**2.** To keep track of the positioning of the blocks, pin a piece of paper labeled "Row 1, Block 1" in the upper left corner of the first block in the first row, again referring to Figure 22. Continue to label each block with its row number and positioning in the row to avoid confusion when stitching.

**3.** Join the blocks together in rows starting at the upper left and working to the right as shown in Figure 23.

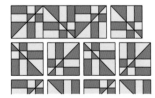

**Figure 23**

**4.** When all rows are stitched, press seams in row 1 in one direction and row 2 in the opposite direction. Continue this sequence for pressing.

**5.** Join the rows in numerical order to complete the pieced center; press all seams in one direction.

### Adding Borders

**1.** Measure across the top and bottom and through the horizontal center of the pieced center to determine the width of the quilt; repeat with sides and vertical center to determine the length of the quilt; write down the measurements. ***Note:*** *If all stitching is precise, the sides should measure 72½", and the top and bottom should measure 48½". We will assume this is the case for cutting border strip sizes.*

**Twist & Turn Quilt**
Placement Diagram 54" x 78"

**2.** Select the I/J inner border fabric strips and stitch right sides together on the short ends with a diagonal seam as shown in Figure 24. Trim seam allowances to ¼" and press seams open, again referring to Figure 24.

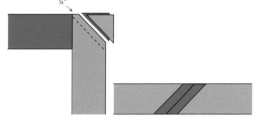

**Figure 24**

**3.** From the joined I/J strip, cut two 72½" J strips and two 50½" I strips.

**4.** Sew the J strips to opposite long sides of the pieced center; press seams toward J strips. Sew the I strips to the top and bottom of the pieced center; press seams toward I strips.

**5.** Repeat step 2 with the K/L outer border strips and then cut two 74½" L strips and two 54½" K strips.

**6.** Sew L strips to opposite long sides and K strips to the top and bottom edges of the pieced center, pressing seams toward L strips and then K strips, to complete the quilt top.

## Completing the Quilt

After the quilt top is pieced, layer the backing, batting and pieced top to make a quilt "sandwich." Pin or baste the layers together and then quilt through all the layers; then bind the edges. Completing the Quilt section on page 29 gives more detail and covers other methods for finishing your quilt.

### Preparing the Quilt Top for Quilting

If you are machine- or hand-quilting the quilt top yourself, follow the instructions below on how to prepare the quilt top for quilting and how to make a quilt sandwich. If you are having your quilt professionally quilted, the longarm quilter (someone who owns a machine specifically made for quilting) will create the quilt sandwich. You only need to give them the backing, batting and pieced top. You will then bind the edges to complete the quilt when you receive it back from them.

**1.** It is easiest to quilt in the ditch of seams (see page 29) or to quilt without a marked pattern by quilting ¼" from seam lines. However, if you prefer to quilt a design on your quilt top, the quilting pattern will have to be marked on the top before layering. Refer to Quilting Designs on page 29 of Construction Techniques for information on design choices and techniques. Then mark your quilting pattern.

**2.** Prepare the backing following suggestions in The Quilt Backing section, page 30, of Completing the Quilt. Press the prepared backing and lay it right side down on the floor. Tape backing edges to the floor with painter's tape, or use T pins if using a carpeted floor or other soft surface.

**3.** Center the batting on the backing and smooth out the wrinkles. *Note: Put the batting in a dryer on low to fluff and lay flat overnight before using to get rid of stubborn fold wrinkles.*

**4.** Lay the quilt top right side up on the batting; smooth out all seams and make sure corners are square.

**5.** Starting in the center of the layers, use quilter's curved safety pins every 6" to hold the layers together, pinning from the center to the edges in every direction. *Note: If you plan to quilt in the ditch of seams, try not to pin close to the seam ditches to avoid having to remove pins as you are quilting.*

**6.** If you prefer, you may hand-baste the layers together starting in the center and working toward the edges in the same manner as using quilter's safety pins. Refer to Sandwiching the Layers on page 31 of Completing the Quilt for more details on layering and basting.

### Quilting

You are now ready to quilt your quilt by hand or machine. See Completing the Quilt section on pages 29–34 for more information about your choices.

### Binding

Binding finishes the edges of your quilt, completing the design. Like a picture frame, your binding can add interest to the overall design or quietly encompass your quilt.

**1.** Join the previously cut 2½"-wide binding strips on the short ends with diagonal seams referring to Figure 25. Trim seams to ¼" and press seams open, again referring to Figure 25.

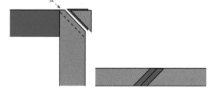

**Figure 25**

**2.** Fold and press the long binding strip wrong sides together to make a double-layered strip as shown in the photo below.

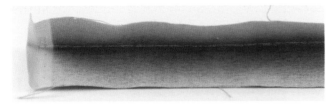

Before applying the binding to your quilt, unfold on one end and fold about a 3" section over in a 45-degree angle with wrong sides together.

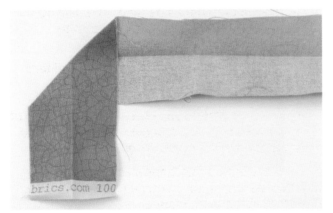

Then fold top down, folding the end of your binding strip so that you create a pocket.

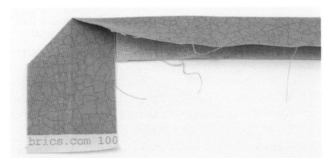

Starting in the middle of a side of your trimmed and squared quilt sandwich, place the binding strip end with the folded pocket, on the right side of the quilt with raw edges together.

Using a ¼" seam allowance, sew along the remaining distance of the side, stopping ¼" from the corner and pivot and make a 45-degree seam to the corner as shown in Figure 26.

**Figure 26**

Fold the binding strip over and up, creating another 45-degree angle as shown in Figure 27. Fold end down and line up with the side. Starting at the top, stitch down the side and repeat the same process at each corner.

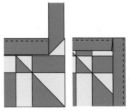

**Figure 27**

### Tips & Techniques

• As you are sewing the binding to your quilt, stop 3" before you get to a corner and mark a dot ¼" in from both directions to make a pivot point for a 45-degree angle at the corner. Don't mark before you have gotten close to the corner.

House of White Birches, Berne, Indiana 46711   Clotilde.com

When you reach the side you started on, stop about 2" before you reach the folded pocket. Line up and pin into place, trim the binding strip at a 45-degree angle so that it will fit into the pocket.

Finish sewing the seam in place.

Trim off the tab even with the edge of the quilt and tuck the end into the pocket.

You are now ready to sew your binding down by hand or machine. *Note: I prefer stitching by hand. It has a much neater look, and as a beginner I would suggest you do your binding this way.* Machine-stitching a binding in place takes a lot of practice.

Begin by slipstitching the front diagonal where the binding ends join.

Turn the binding to the back side of the quilt and slipstitch edges in place to cover the raw edge and seam line.

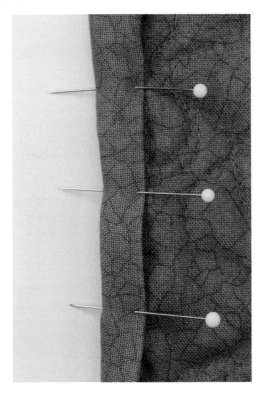

Congratulations! You have completed your first quilt. ❖

House of White Birches, Berne, Indiana 46711   Clotilde.com

# Pattern & Fabric Selection

## Choosing a Pattern

The quiltmaking journey usually begins with the selection of a pattern. Often inspiration comes from a quilting magazine or book. Or sometimes, you see a fabric, and just like that, you know you want to use it in a quilt.

Choose a quilting pattern with a comprehensive list of fabrics, and clear cutting and assembly instructions. It should also list the skill level required to complete the quilt.

As a true beginner, you should not select an intermediate or advanced pattern no matter how much you love it! Save those more difficult patterns until you develop your skills to a level where you will be able to successfully complete the project. If you start with a project beyond your skill level, you may run into problems that will discourage you to the point of not finishing that quilt and never starting another one. Your quiltmaking journey would be over before it has a chance to begin.

Take the pattern you have chosen with you when you go shopping for fabric. You will want to look at the photos and drawings to see how the fabrics work together. You will also need the supply list provided to tell you how much fabric you need to buy.

As a beginner, you probably don't have much of a fabric stash (fabrics on hand), so you will have to purchase all that is required for the quilt.

If quilting becomes a passion for you, you will soon find out just what a fabric stash is and how enthusiastic quilters can get about collecting fabrics.

The pattern chosen for this book, Twist & Turn Quilt made with 24 Ollie's Square blocks, requires just two fabrics—a light and a dark for the blocks and the outer borders, and a contrasting fabric for the narrow inner borders. For the binding you may use the same dark fabric as used in the blocks, or choose another coordinating dark fabric. The amount of fabric needed for the binding is given separately from other fabric. All the cutting for this pattern can be done with a rotary cutter, and the piecing is done with all straight seams. The hardest part of the whole construction process is deciding on the layout of the blocks when putting them together to complete the pieced center.

Once you have finished this quilt, you will be on your way to choosing lots of patterns you will want to try. Taking classes at quilt shows and local quilt shops will help add new skills to your quilting resumé. Before you know it, you will be hooked.

## Fabric Selection

For your first quilt, keep it simple. The block pattern we have selected for your first quilt requires just two fabrics with good contrast or a light fabric and a dark fabric. This will ensure a happy ending to your first quilt experience.

Fabric selection is one of the most important parts of quilting. Color, scale, texture and your taste should all be considered when making your selections. For example, when making a quilt as a decorator accent for a room, the worst thing you can do is work with color paint chips first. Instead, go to your quilt shop with an open mind. Let the fabrics inspire you. It's much easier to have paint mixed than to limit yourself with color choices in the fabric selections. Pick your fabrics first, and then match the paint color. It will save you a lot of aggravation if you keep an open mind to the possibilities for your project.

With the block pattern we are using, you will need two fabrics for the body of the quilt. Then you will need one more fabric for the narrow inner border. The outer border for this project should be cut from the same focus fabric (the dark fabric) used in the blocks. You may want to wait to purchase the fabric for the inner border until after you see your blocks together. Often, the blocks do not look just the way you pictured them in your mind's eye.

Sometimes you may find you need to incorporate a third accent color to the mix. And then again, sometimes you may choose to only use one border or possibly no border at all. A quilt will tell you what it needs, so listen to it.

When selecting your fabric for the blocks, keep in mind that you need high contrast or dark and light in your two choices to make the pattern pop out. If the fabrics are too similar in tone, you will not see the design. Look at the quilts in the Gallery

*This quilt is just one option for the Twist & Turn. Notice that it has only an outer border and contrasting binding.*

of Quilts section on page 38 to see the difference fabric selection can make.

A nice medium-to-dark print with a lighter tonal or solid makes a great first quilt, and it's safe. When in doubt, go safe—at least for your first quilt.

Audition several fabric selections. Find three or four fabrics you think you would like as your main fabric and then look for secondary fabrics that will complement them. Keep an open mind. Once you have made your tentative selections, there are a few questions you need to ask.

### Is the Fabric Directional?

If your fabric is directional, that is, if it has a nap, or print with an "up" and "down," how will it look in the block and the quilt? If there is diagonal piecing in your blocks or pattern, (our blocks do have bias—diagonally cut pieces) this is something you need to consider when cutting the pieces. How will the direction of the fabric print work if used on the diagonal? Also, if your fabric has a directional motif—flower vases, for example—do you want some of them upside down?

### Does Your Fabric Have Texture?

Some textures do not go well together. If you are using textures really look at them. It's not just

about the color; sometimes, you need to pay close attention to how the fabrics "feel" together. You wouldn't put a white snowflake flannel fabric with a summer textural green grass fabric, even though white and green go together well. First, flannel and quilters cotton shouldn't be mixed. They have different thread counts and shrink at different rates and second, snowflakes and grass are two themes you wouldn't normally put together.

### Does Your Fabric Have a Theme?

If you like traditional patterns and traditional fabrics then stick with the style you like. The block pattern in this book is considered a traditional design. You can choose traditional-looking fabrics, but the pattern works well with contemporary-style fabrics too. The great thing about traditional block and quilt patterns is that they are adaptable to different tastes and styles. Your sense of style is the guiding factor, so be true to what you like. Not everyone is meant to follow the trends. It is important that you like the fabrics you are working with. If you like fun and funky colors, use them. If you like to decorate with Americana, select colors and prints that go with that theme. But if you are doing fun and funky colors don't mix them with Americana-style fabrics. The two styles are not compatible.

House of White Birches, Berne, Indiana 46711   Clotilde.com

### Are You Using a Lot of Different Color Tones?

Having a color wheel is helpful when trying to make color decisions. Not all greens go together. The same is true for all colors. Think of fabric colors as you would paints. If you want green, you mix blue and yellow together. Depending on how much yellow you add, the color will change to lime. If you add black to the mix you will get olive. If you think of fabrics in terms of mixing paints you will start to see why certain colors do not look right together. For the most part, you will know something is not quite right. Trust your instincts.

Colors that are diluted with grays, blacks and whites are tricky to coordinate. You need to really look at the tone and think about how it was made. For example, pink is made using red and white. If you add gray you get mauve. A bright pink will not look good with a mauve, but a dusty rose will. Why? A dusty rose has a touch of gray in it, which softens it. Mauve is also a subtle color; a bright pink would clash with a mauve. So when you pick your fabrics, pay close attention to the tone.

### How Does It Feel to You?

Sometimes you can find the perfect color combinations and still not feel right about them. Usually this happens when you are trying to match a wonderful fabric, one that you just love. Color is not the only consideration. For example, if you are working on a quilt using Civil War reproduction fabrics, you wouldn't use a contemporary print with them. Or perhaps you have an Asian-theme collection, and you need a brown to go with it. You wouldn't use a juvenile print, even if the color is right. The style of the fabric also dictates how it is used. I will say, that on occasion, I have actually used and have also seen fabrics that shouldn't have gone together that really did work. There are always exceptions to every rule. It is a judgment call at the end of the day. There is no absolute set of rules. Sometimes fabrics just feel wrong together, and then again, sometimes they speak to each other.

### Is There Enough Contrast?

If you have trouble determining if there is enough contrast between your fabrics, the best thing to do is to buy a color wheel. Color is something that scares new quilters and yet color should be the most fun. Picking out your colors and fabrics, and watching the quilt come together, is what it is all about. Most new quilters think there is a magic potion to help them select the perfect fabrics. What it boils down to is: Do you like it? At the end of the day, it is your quilt. If you like the colors you have selected, that is all that matters.

### Do You Want to Use a Fabric Collection?

Collections are great for the new quilter. The fabrics in a collection all match, and you don't have to do much thinking, but they can also present a problem. Many collections contain medium tones and don't allow for the lights and darks that make most patterns pop. Sometimes they don't have a main print around which all the other fabrics are created.

If you like the shabby chic look, you will love working within collections. And just because you find a fabric you love in a collection, doesn't mean you can't combine it with another fabric from a different collection. There are a lot of basic fabric lines that offer the contrast and color range you might need. Don't limit yourself by failing to look all around your local quilt shop. Really see the possibilities. Picking your fabric is an important part of the process. Know your options and don't be afraid to play around.

Once you have made your decision as to fabrics, color and pattern, then the real work begins.

## Understanding Fabric

There is a lot to learn about fabric from the way it is made to how to cut it for use in your projects. Depending on the project and its use, a good practice is to purchase the best quality fabric available. That doesn't mean that you should buy very expensive fabric to make a Halloween costume that will be worn once, but when making a quilt that should last a lifetime, using the best quality fabric is a good investment.

It helps to know a little about how fabric is woven because the grain of the fabric and its placement is important. This determines how the fabric is cut. Cutting is a technique to be mastered, and after selecting and preparing the fabric, it's a crucial first step in the quiltmaking process.

### Fabric Grain

Fabric is made from weaving threads together horizontally and vertically on a loom. The horizontal or vertical directions that the threads run are called the grain. The horizontal grain is called the crosswise grain; the vertical grain is called the lengthwise grain (see Figure 1). Strips are usually cut along the straight of grain, that is, they are cut the same direction that the grain runs.

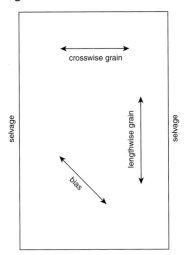

**Figure 1**

The term bias refers to the diagonal of the fabric (see Figure 1). If you are cutting a square diagonally, you are cutting on the bias. Bias will also stretch.

The selvage is the finished edge of the fabric (see Figure 1). In the store, the width measurement given is the total width that includes the selvages. For the purpose of quilting, the width of the fabric is measured from the inside of the selvage on one side to the inside of the selvage on the opposite side; this area is called the "usable width."

The most common way to cut strips is on the cross-grain—from selvage to selvage.

Textile companies use the selvage-edge space to add the name and also the color dots of the shades used in the fabric. These color dots are a great guide for knowing just what colors have been used in printing your fabrics. You can always use these dots to help pick color coordinates.

## Tips & Techniques

• *It is a good idea to always press your fabric before you begin to cut. A flat, unwrinkled fabric will cut much more accurately.*

## Preparing Fabric for Cutting

The first thing you must do before you begin to cut out your quilt pieces is to make sure the fabric is cut straight with the grain. Just because a fabric is folded in half doesn't mean that it is straight. If the fabric is not straight at the ends, you need to straighten it before cutting.

To do this, press your fabric flat. Fold it in half lengthwise, holding at the fold and sliding the fabric until the selvage ends are equal on both end lengths of the selvage.

More specific cutting instructions are given in Cutting the Fabric and Using a Rotary Cutter, both found on page 22.

## Tips & Techniques

• *Anchor your ruler in place and keep your fingers out of the area of cutting by placing your little finger on the mat (off the ruler). This will keep your ruler secure and, at the same time, force you to keep your fingers out of the way. You will have fewer mistakes in cutting because your ruler will not slide.*

## To Wash or Not to Wash

Personally, I do not prewash my fabrics, but I will also be the first to tell you that you should. I have been very lucky, and in the 10 years I have been quilting I have never had an issue with dye running or uneven shrinkage. I do, however, always use quality fabrics, and I always use a color fixative the first time I wash a quilt. I also make it a practice to provide washing instructions with each quilt I give away.

If you chose to prewash your fabrics make sure all the fabrics that will be used in the project are prewashed.

Another good practice—do not mix poor-quality fabrics with good-quality fabrics. For the most part, the greige goods (quality of the fabric it is printed on) are different, which means they will shrink at different percentages and possibly unevenly on the same piece of fabric. If you are using good-quality fabrics, use all good-quality fabrics. ❖

# Supplies & Tools for Quiltmaking

Because of the popularity of quilting, supplies and tools have been developed especially for quilters, by quilters. Many of these are necessary, while others are fun to add to your collection. The following sections cover the necessary supplies and tools every quilter should have on hand.

## Quiltmaking Supplies

### Thread

If using predominately cotton fabrics, cotton thread is recommended. I have my favorites, but this is really a question of personal taste. I would suggest that you use synthetic threads very sparingly. I only use them in art quilts. Synthetic threads are stronger than the cotton we use, and friction will cause them to wear through the cotton faster.

A neutral-color thread is recommended for piecing. It is difficult to find thread that will match both the light and dark fabrics used in a quilt. A good neutral color would be gray, tan or dark tan. These colors will blend with almost any color.

Sewing machines seem to have their own likes and dislikes when it comes to thread. Try different brands and types of thread to see which one works best with your machine.

## Batting

There are lots of batting choices for quilters today. Manufacturers have improved battings to allow quilters more freedom in the quilting process.

Whether you will be quilting sparingly or stipple-quilting in every square inch, there is a batting that is perfect for your choice. Read the information provided on the batting package to find out about the recommended quilting density before purchase.

The only way to find your personal favorites is to try them out. You can examine and feel the quilts others have made to find the types that most appeal to your tactile sense, and then try them out on a small project before using them in a larger quilt.

Batting can make or break a quilt, so selecting the perfect one for your project is an important decision. The fibers used in today's battings range from 100 percent cotton to 100 percent polyester and everything in between. Earth-friendly choices, such as quickly renewable bamboo, are being introduced to the batting blends.

**Polyester batting:** This type of batting tends to be thicker and warmer because it does not breathe. Quilting designs show up well in the loft. When machine-quilting on a quilt made with polyester batting, it has a tendency to move around. It launders nicely and does not shrink or lose its shape. It is easy to hand-quilt because the fibers are slippery. It resists mold and mildew.

**Cotton batting:** This natural-fiber batting is warm, and it breathes. It is very easy to quilt through and washes beautifully. It softens with age. Today, cotton battings are bonded to hold the fibers together so they don't lump when washed. Some cotton battings will shrink; read the label before using.

**Cotton-poly blends:** Blended cotton-and-polyester batting is less expensive than 100 percent cotton. The ratio of cotton to polyester varies from one brand to another. This type of batting is warm and is easy to quilt.

**Silk batting:** Silk batting is the most expensive batting out there, but it's wonderful to work with. It is a good alternative to wool. It is lightweight, warm and very soft.

**Wool batting:** Wool makes a very warm batting without adding weight. It is very easy to quilt through. It absorbs moisture, making it a good choice for cool, damp climates. It is more expensive than cotton and polyester. Some wool battings are

washable, so read the label before buying. And remember, some people are allergic to wool.

**Bamboo batting:** This is the new kid on the block. Results are equally good whether the quilting is done by hand or on a home machine or longarm machine. It washes well. Commonly made of a blend of 50 percent naturally antibacterial bamboo fiber and 50 percent organic cotton, it is soft and supple with excellent loft and a thin scrim (a loosely woven fabric used to contain the fibers), making it perfect for machine quilting. It is also the choice of those quilters who want to use a product that is ecologically sound.

## Tools of the Trade

There are many great tools, supplies and gadgets on the market that will help you in your pursuit of quilting.

Here you will find a basic list of helpful tools for the beginner, or even the seasoned quilter, to use on a day-to-day basis for machine piecing and quilting.

### Sewing Machine

For quilting, it is not necessary to run out and buy a top-of-the-line $4,000 sewing machine. There are many good machines on the market that will do the job for around $300.

You can always upgrade in the future if you find that quilting is your passion. You really don't need a machine with all the bells and whistles on it for quilting.

A machine with a straight and a zigzag stitch with good thread tension is the most important. If you are going to buy a new machine, look for one with the needle down feature. This feature can be helpful, especially if appliqué is in your future.

### Sewing Machine Needles

For piecing on the sewing machine, it is best to use a smaller-size needle. I have found that a Microtex 10/70 sharp is the best all-around needle for the sewing I do. It is the perfect needle for piecing and for quilting.

I do, however, change to a Microtex 8/60 when I do fusible appliqué with batik fabric. It leaves a much smaller hole and the finished stitch looks much neater.

The 90/14 needle, which is listed as a quilting needle, is larger and will break the thread in your fabric from time to time.

Never use a ball-point needle for piecing or quilting. These needles are made especially for sewing on knits and some stretch fabrics, but not woven quilting fabrics. These have a rounded tip and will break cotton fibers as you sew.

### Rulers

Quilting rulers are used for both measuring and cutting. There are three sizes I would suggest as must-haves—4½" x 12", 6½" x 24" and 12½" square.

When buying rulers, look at the markings and size increments. Some have only ¼" increments, while others include ⅛" increments. Many patterns require the ⅛" measurement, so it is best to purchase rulers that include those increments.

They are available in several colors, and I find some of them difficult to read. Some rulers have yellow lines, others have green lines and still others have black lines. I find the black lettering and markings most versatile for all colors of fabric. One color may work better for you than another, depending on your eyesight.

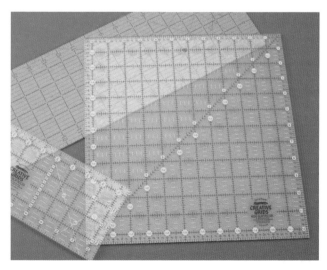

### Rotary Cutter

For accurate cutting, a rotary cutter is a definite must-have. There are several types to choose from; find the one you like best.

I'm not overly fond of ergonomic cutters, finding them hard to work with. For myself, I prefer the very plain cutters, but that is a personal decision. If you have an opportunity, try out a few types to see what feels best in your hand.

The best size of rotary cutter to own, in my opinion, is the 45mm size. If you are working with small pieces for a miniature quilt, a smaller cutter made especially for this purpose might work best for you.

Safety is very important for any rotary cutter. Be sure yours has a lock to keep the blade from turning when it's not in use.

### Cutting Mat

When purchasing a cutting mat, consider the space you have to work with. The best size cutting mat to buy is 24" x 36"; however, you must have a flat surface to accommodate it. Most people end up purchasing the next size down—18" x 24". The problem with the smaller mat is that you must fold your fabric in quarters to cut width-of-fabric strips. If the fabric is not folded correctly, you will get a "wave" in your strip. This can cause problems when piecing.

Purchase the largest mat you can. Look for a soft surface, self-healing mat, instead of the hard plastic ones. You will use fewer rotary blades with a soft mat because the blades will stay sharp longer.

Cutting mats are marked just like a ruler. They can be used as guides for cutting strips, but whenever possible, use a rotary-cutting ruler to cut sizes.

### Fabric Markers

Fabric markers are used to transfer quilting designs and other pattern markings to fabric. It is important that these marks are visible while working on a project but can be removed when the quilt is complete.

I like a marker with replaceable leads in different colors. These leads do not leave marks on your projects and can be erased easily with the attached eraser.

I also like water-soluble markers for ease of removal. All you have to do is spritz with water and the marks disappear. How easy is that?

Either one of these types of markers is a necessary tool for quilting.

## Straight Pins & Binding Clips
Pins should be fine so they don't leave large holes in your fabric. They should be long enough to take a big bite of fabric when inserted. They should be rustproof.

Silk pins are great. Buy pins with glass heads so they don't melt when pressing. One of the best brands is Clotilde's IBC glass pins, available at Clotilde.com. The plastic pins will melt and

sometimes the ends come off, not to mention that they can ruin your iron.

Do not leave pins in fabrics for long periods of time—they could cause damage.

Binding clips are also useful and easy to use at edges that need to be held together (these are also available at Clotilde.com).

## Safety Pins
Safety pins are used for pin basting. You will want to purchase either brass- or nickel-plated pins, so if they are left in the fabric for any length of time they will not rust and create stains. You can also purchase curved safety pins. These are designed to make it easier to pin on a flat surface.

## Scissors
A good, sharp pair of scissors or shears is a must. They don't have to be dressmaker shears, but they do need to be a good quality. I use 4" embroidery scissors for almost everything. When you use a rotary cutter, there isn't a need for anything bigger most of the time.

If cutting individual pieces for appliqué or for template piecing, you will find your own preference as to the sizes needed. It helps to keep a pair handy while at the sewing machine and at the cutting table.

## Iron & Ironing Board
You will need a good iron and a large flat surface for pressing. You may consider purchasing a large board, 59" x 22", that will fit over your ironing board to make it possible to iron a wide width of fabric. As you add to your quilting tools and supplies, this large ironing surface is a good investment.

A good steam/dry iron is all you need to start quilting. Be sure it is clean and ready to use.

## Seam Ripper
Unfortunately, a seam ripper is a necessary tool. On occasion we must undo our sewing. Be very careful when using a seam ripper. It is easy to slip and cut fabric instead of thread.

## Good Lighting
When cutting and sewing, it is absolutely crucial to have good lighting. Position lighting so that it casts the least amount of shadows on your work surface or sewing machine. When cutting and sewing, you must be able to read measurements and stitch an accurate ¼" seam allowance. ❖

House of White Birches, Berne, Indiana 46711   Clotilde.com

# Cutting Your Fabric Using a Rotary Cutter

## Cutting the Fabric

We are using rotary-cutting techniques to cut the pieces for the Twist & Turn quilt. Some quilts require templates with individual cutting instructions. Other quilts include appliqué pieces, which cannot be rotary-cut. Rotary cutting is the easiest and fastest method to use to cut the pieces needed for a quilt.

Rotary cutting can be dangerous. Safety is a crucial issue when using a rotary cutter. Be very careful and pay close attention to what you are doing around a rotary cutter. Do not leave them open when not in use.

### Tools for Rotary Cutting

For the best results, use a rotary cutter and a 24" x 36" self-healing mat to cut out quilt pieces. You will also need quilters' rulers. The most common and useful sizes are: 4½" x 12", 6½" x 24½" and a 12½"-square ruler. These are the basic cutting tools to get you started. There are many specialty rulers and gadgets, but as a beginner you will be using basic rotary-cutting tools.

## Using a Rotary Cutter

To make a good straight cut with a rotary cutter, it is best to hold the cutter at a 45-degree angle so that you have some weight behind the blade, but not too much. If you hold the handle too close to the mat, you will not have enough pressure on the blade to make the cut, and if you hold it straight up, you will not have the control you need.

**For safety, always cut away from you. Never cut toward you.** Remember that a rotary cutter is very sharp, and if you keep a good blade in it, there is little need to push down hard. If it becomes difficult to cut, or you get a lot of skips, it is time to change the blade. Never use it like a saw, going back and forth. That is when accidents happen and pieces are cut incorrectly.

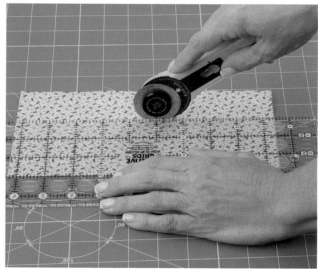

*Holding rotary cutter correctly.*

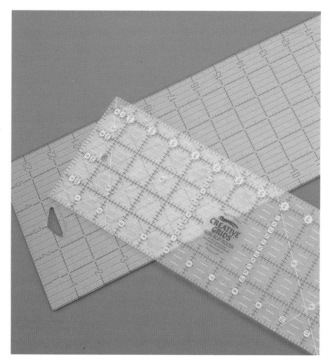

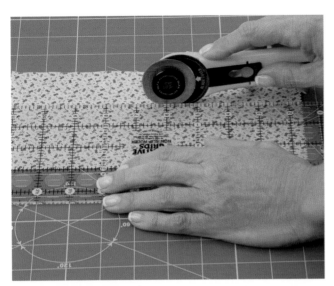

*Holding rotary cutter too low.*

*Holding rotary cutter too high.*

## Preparing Fabric for Cutting

The first thing you must do before you begin to cut out your quilt pieces is to make sure the fabric is cut straight with the grain. Just because a fabric is folded in half doesn't mean that it is straight. If the fabric is not straight, you need to straighten it before cutting.

To do this, press your fabric flat. Fold it in half lengthwise, holding at the fold and sliding the fabric until the selvage ends are equal on both end lengths of the selvage.

## Cutting Strips

When you have your fabric even and are ready to begin, lay the folded piece on your cutting mat with the fold aligned with a single line on your mat as shown in Figure 1. For the sake of accuracy, you will only use the lines on your ruler for measuring to cut your strips. As you gain experience, you will learn more ways to make the best use of your cutting mat and all its lines.

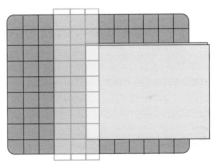

**Figure 1**

If you notice in the quoted instructions below, it reads "Cut two 6⅞" by fabric width strips." This means we will be cutting 6⅞" strips from the piece that you aligned on your mat. But before we begin to cut, we first must address the size of the strip and also straighten the fabric along the edge you are cutting.

"Cut two 6⅞" by fabric width strips light fabric; subcut strips into (12) 6⅞" squares. Cut each square in half on one diagonal to make a total of 24 A triangles."

Using a line on your mat, from fold to selvage, trim the raw edge. This will be the edge you will measure from when cutting your strips.

Always cut a strip with one ruler when possible; there is less chance for a mistake. If you do not have a ruler that is wide enough for the strip you need, you will need to butt two rulers together to make the cut.

For example, if you need to cut 6⅞" strips and only have a 6"-wide ruler, you will need to place one ruler along the straightened side edge ⅞" in, making sure to line it up from top to bottom. Lay the 6" x 24" ruler next to that ruler, making sure not to move the ruler you first placed down. You should now have a measurement of 6⅞" and can cut the strip, remembering to cut away from your body, not toward your body (Figure 2).

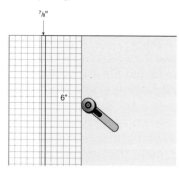

**Figure 2**

### Subcutting the Strips

The second part of the sentence of the cutting instructions says, "subcut strips into (12) 6⅞" squares."

"Subcut" means to go back to the two 6⅞"-wide strips you just cut, and measure and cut those strips again at 6⅞" increments to make a total of 12 squares that measure 6⅞" on each side (Figure 3). Remember that your fabric is folded in half so each time you make a cut you are cutting two squares. Subcut one strip at a time for better accuracy.

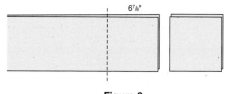

**Figure 3**

The last step of the cutting instructions says to "Cut each square in half on one diagonal to make a total of 24 A triangles." When you have 12 squares cut, you will then cut them diagonally from corner to corner to make triangles (Figure 4), which we have labeled A. Do not cut more than a pair at a time. Line the ruler up from corner to corner, taking extra caution by double-checking placement before cutting.

**Figure 4**

You are now ready to continue on with your cutting. Go one step at a time and remember, measure twice and cut once! ❖

## Tips & Techniques

• *Cut one fabric at a time, label each different cut, especially triangles.*

• *Once cut, it is hard to identify the pieces. Sticky notes work perfectly for this purpose.*

# Construction Techniques

## Piecing a Quilt

Sewing pieces together to make blocks or units is what quilters call piecing. Even appliqué quilts incorporate piecing at some stage.

Some quilters prefer to hand-piece. This is a time-consuming process, but for some it is a restful, peaceful way to make a quilt.

There are those of us who prefer to make quilts in less time. We love to use our sewing machines to piece quilts.

Just because we like to work faster doesn't mean we want to sacrifice accuracy. There are some special techniques that will help reduce the number of mistakes and help guarantee accuracy when piecing.

## Piecing

If you are making a quilt you are piecing. Quilters take big pieces of fabric and cut them into little pieces to sew them into big pieces again. That is quilting.

If you noticed that all the cutting sizes given for the sample quilt have fractions, that's because in quilting piecing is done with ¼" seams. Having uniform seams throughout your quilt helps with accuracy.

Straight piecing is what you will be doing most of the time in quilting, especially as a beginner. Straight piecing is working along the straight of grain, which is more stable and doesn't stretch.

When piecing, two pieces of fabric are placed with right sides together, matching the edges to be stitched. There is no need to reverse stitches at the beginning and end when you are machine stitching because almost all seams will be stitched over, but many quilters like to backstitch a few stitches (particularly when they are hand-stitching) just to lock the seam so it won't come out later.

If you want to backstitch on your machine, you should start stitching about ⅛" from the edge of the seam, backstitch and then stitch forward until the end of the seam, stitching a perfect ¼" seam allowance along the length of the seam. When you reach the end of the seam, backstitch a few stitches.

Chain piecing is a term used for piecing a large number of the same pieces in an unbroken chain.

It saves a lot of thread and time. It also eliminates a lot of running back and forth to the ironing board. Chain piecing is actually preferred by seasoned quilters.

Chain piecing allows the quiltmaker to make units for a large number of blocks at the same time, instead of piecing one block at a time.

Begin chain piecing as for straight stitching, except when you finish stitching one unit, immediately add another unit without stopping to cut the thread as shown in Figure 1. When you have finished stitching all identical units, cut the thread and cut the units apart. Then press the units as directed in the pattern instructions.

**Figure 1**

## Achieving an Accurate Seam Allowance

The standard seam allowance used in all quilting patterns is ¼". This allows room for stability, minimal bulk at intersections and easy pressing. If you are to have accurate-size blocks, you must have accurate ¼" seams. There is nothing more important in piecing than the seams. If the seam allowance is off, the entire quilt will be off. To make your quilt fit together right, you must have your seam allowances consistent. It's mathematics, plain and simple.

The easiest way to sew an accurate ¼" seam is with a ¼" foot for your sewing machine. If your machine doesn't have a special ¼" foot, check with your local machine dealer or online at websites such as Clotilde.com for a ¼" foot. This type of foot is available for all sewing-machine models, old and new.

Other ways to get a perfect ¼" seam include using masking tape on your machine to mark the ¼" seam allowance. There are also guides that can be placed on your machine's table to set at certain measurements.

Some sewing machines allow you to move the needle. If your machine is one of those, you can move the needle so it is ¼" away from the edge of the presser foot, allowing you to use the presser-foot edge as the guide for sewing perfect ¼" seams.

## Construction Terminology

**Nesting Seams** —Nesting seams is how you get seams to match up. To nest your seams you first need to make sure you pressed properly. The two sections you're putting together need to be pressed in different directions so that when pushed together you have a high side on each side of the seam. Just push the seams together until they are snug and pin as shown in Figure 2.

**Figure 2**

**Dog Ears**—Dog ears are the extra pieces hanging over the seams of diagonal-pieced units. These need to be clipped off so they don't interfere with the 1/4" seams. Use the block edge as the trimming guide as shown in Figure 3.

**Figure 3**

## Pressing

Pressing is an important part of the quilting process. Pressing correctly will help with your accuracy when piecing and with the assembly of the blocks.

### Press Fabrics Before Cutting

If you make sure your fabric is pressed and wrinkle free before cutting, you will get a better cut. Even the folds from the way your fabric was folded or stored can cause miscuts. Always make sure your fabric is flat and smooth before you begin. In this case, you may need to use steam, or mist the fabric with a spray bottle filled with water before ironing, to remove stubborn wrinkles.

### With or Without Steam

It is recommended you not use steam when pressing seams. Steam will stretch your fabric if not used properly, so it is best not to use it when piecing until you learn how to press without distorting the fabric.

### Press After Each Step

Press after each assembly step. Don't wait for a couple of steps. Make the trip to the ironing board each time you finish a seam or chain-pieced seams.

### How to Press Seams

Most of the time, seams are pressed toward the darker fabric piece. However, this doesn't work for all patterns. It is good to assemble one entire block before making a larger number of blocks so that you know which way to press. Doing this will save you a lot of time re-pressing later as you assemble the rest of the blocks.

Often it is easier to press a seam toward the side that doesn't include other seams as shown in Figure 4. So, if you have a rectangle being stitched to several pieced units, it makes sense to press the seams toward the rectangle no matter what the color.

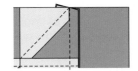

**Figure 4**

Sometimes it is difficult to make pressing decisions. For example, if one single block design is used to make an entire quilt and all the blocks are placed in the same position in the rows, then the seams of the blocks in one row should be pressed in the opposite direction from the seams in the next row of blocks. This is when pressing can get complicated, and planning pressing in advance is very important.

Absolutely do not wiggle the iron when pressing. Just as steam distorts the fabric, so does wiggling. To press a seam, simply make sure both seams are facing in the same direction as stated in the instructions, and then iron in that direction without wiggling. If you run the hot iron up to and over the seam, it will open fully and lay nice and flat.

## Block Construction
Most blocks are stitched in units, which are then pressed and joined with other units to make rows. The pieces in the Ollie's Square blocks used in the sample quilt were stitched in units. The units were joined in rows, and the rows were joined to complete the blocks.

Letters are assigned to block pieces for cutting and for ease of reference in later instructions. This eliminates the need for instructions to include sizes and fabric colors in constant repetition in patterns.

It helps to sort pieces into piles and label the piles with the appropriate letter. This type of organization helps develop good habits for future quilting. In time, some things will be automatic, so learning good habits right from the start is a big help later on.

## Square-Up the Blocks
After the blocks are assembled, they need to be measured to be sure they are a consistent size.

In a perfect world, all of the blocks for the Twist & Turn Quilt should measure 12½" on each side. Don't get upset if the blocks are not all consistent in size. Most of the time, blocks will vary a bit. Even blocks pieced by experienced quilters are sometimes off a bit.

Lay a 12½" square ruler on top of each block to see how you did. If there is a lot of difference between the blocks, you may have to "square down" the size to the smallest block. This must be done carefully so as not to lose the points on any triangle piecing.

When trimming, distribute the excess evenly, trimming off a bit from all sides. You want to keep the block design centered.

There is a bit of a "fudge factor" in quilting. Sometimes with just a little pull here or there, blocks will fit together.

## Putting It All Together

### Choosing a Layout
Once the blocks are made and squared to a consistent size, it is time to decide on how you would like to set them together.

The Twist & Turn Quilt is constructed with only one block design. The block can be placed in different positions to create different patterns. It will be fun to explore your options.

You may discover an arrangement for your blocks that hasn't been done before. You will find that working with traditional block designs is a real source of inspiration.

There are many different ways to set your blocks. We are using only one block pattern and turning it, but think of the possibilities if you use two or three different blocks.

Lay your blocks out on the floor and rotate them in different directions until you start to see the possibilities. There are two obvious patterns that happen. Double Diamonds and Reversed Stripes (see the Alternate Placement Diagrams on pages 43–47.

### Assemble the Quilt Top
Once you have decided how you want to set the blocks, it's time to assemble them into rows. Pin the blocks together in rows, pinning at each unit intersection and between, making sure to match seams perfectly.

Sew the blocks together from left to right to make the rows, beginning with the top row, removing pins as you stitch. Repeat the same procedure for each row.

When all rows are assembled, press seams in adjoining rows in opposite directions, and then pin and sew the first row to the second, add the third to the second, and continue until all rows are attached. Press seams in one direction.

### Tips & Techniques

*• A little trick that you can do that will save you from "unsewing" is to use a sticky note to label the rows—row 1, row 2, etc. It is easy to mix up the rows while attaching them together, and unfortunately, that leads to having to rip out your sewing. This tip will save you a lot of frustration.*

### Square-Up the Quilt Center

Now that the blocks are assembled to make the quilt top, it's time to see how we did. We need to measure the quilt top to see if it is square.

Measure the width from side to side, through the center and at the top and bottom. When the measurement is off from side to side, we take the middle measurement (which will usually be a bit bigger) and cut our top and bottom borders to that size. For example, if the top width measures 50½", the center width is 50¾", and the bottom width measures 50¼", the top and the bottom border need to be cut at 50¾". When it is pinned in place, it is easy to ease in the ½".

Use the same technique to measure the length of the quilt from the top to the bottom for the side borders.

### Making & Adding Borders

Sometimes border strips have to be cut along the length of the fabric. This is especially true if a border print is used that has an upright, directional design and is printed along the length. In this case, there is often a lot of fabric left over.

When possible, border strips are pieced from strips cut across the width of the fabric. These strips are cut diagonally on the short ends and then joined. The seams are pressed open as shown in Figure 5, and then the strips are cut to the required lengths.

**Figure 5**

Once the borders are constructed, they are added to the quilt top in the order given in the instructions, often sides first and then top and bottom.

Mark the center of each border strip length and center points of each quilt side. Match border center to quilt side center as shown in Figure 6. Pin borders to quilt top at each end and in the center. Then pin from the center to the ends, easing or pulling a little as necessary to make fit. Stitch the border to the quilt top and press the seam toward border. The same is done to all sides as you add each border strip.

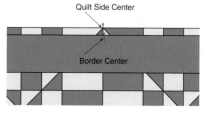

**Figure 6**

After adding the first (inner) border strips and pressing, the quilt should now be square and ready for the addition of a second (outer) border. Measure and cut the side, top and bottom strips for the second border to size and attach in the same manner.

Once all the borders are in place it is time to give your finished top a thorough pressing. Remember now, NO iron wiggling! ❖

# Completing the Quilt

Although this book is about learning to piece quilts, we can't ignore the quilting process. Once the quilt top is pieced, it must be prepared for quilting and finishing. Quilting is the glue that holds your quilt together. You can do it yourself by hand or on a regular sewing machine, or you can take your quilt to a professional for quilting on a longarm machine.

If you do the quilting yourself, you will need to decide on the method you want to use and choose a quilting design before sandwiching the quilt top, batting and backing layers together.

## Hand or Sewing-Machine Quilting

### Designs
Quilting stitches can follow the seam lines of the pieced blocks, (called stitching in the ditch) or worked in a decorative design to add beauty to a finished quilt. It is necessary to have a plan for your design.

Some methods involve marking the design on the quilt top. This must be done before the quilt layers are sandwiched together. The designs should be drawn on with a water-soluble marker, chalk or pencil that can be erased. The design marks must be clearly visible during quilting, but be completely removed afterward and not show on the finished quilt. Here are some of the many design choices available.

### Quilting in the Ditch
In-the-ditch quilting is the most common form of quilting for beginners. It can be done by hand or machine. There is no need to mark anything on the quilt top when using this method.

A walking foot may be used, replacing the foot currently on the sewing machine. This foot allows the machine to grab the fabric on both the top and bottom layers to keep them together. This helps avoid fabric bunching at the end of the stitching and keeps the layers smooth.

If you prefer that the thread does not show or can't find a color you like, you may use a clear or transparent polyester thread in the top of the machine.

Stitching in the ditch is stitching on the low side of seams—the side without the seam allowance behind it. After you have tried this technique you will know one of the reasons why pressing during piecing is so important.

### Crosshatch Quilting
Crosshatching can be done either by hand or machine. You can mark the diagonal lines on the quilt top using a water-soluble marker, or you can use painter's tape as a guide for stitching.

To use painter's tape, simply lay it in place as desired and stitch along the edge. This serves two purposes—you get a nice straight line every time, and you have a sewing guide. After stitching on both sides of the tape, pick it up and reposition it next to the seam you just stitched and repeat. The tape can be used over and over again. This saves time in marking, and you don't have to worry about removing the marks when the quilting is finished.

Do not leave tape on your quilt top when you are not stitching. Even painter's tape could leave sticky residue on the quilt top over time that would be hard to remove.

House of White Birches, Berne, Indiana 46711  Clotilde.com

### Free-Motion Quilting

For free-motion quilting, you need to disengage the feed dogs on your sewing machine; this allows the fabric to be moved freely on the sewing bed. The length of the stitches is determined by the directional movement of the fabric between the up and down needle motion. You will get smaller stitches by moving slowly and longer stitches by moving quickly.

A free-motion foot, darning foot or quilting foot may be used, depending on your machine. You can stitch in any direction—forward, backward, left or right. Consistent free-motion quilting takes practice, but once you have mastered it, you can quilt using many different motifs. You are only limited by your own imagination.

If you will use this method often, you must maintain good posture. This type of quilting can be tiring for the arms, shoulders and back.

### Stipple Quilting

Stippling is a form of free-motion quilting. Stippling is scribbling with thread on fabric. Usually it looks like puzzle pieces, but it can also be loops.

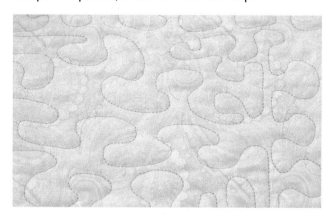

### Purchased Quilting Designs

There are entire books filled with quilting designs. You may choose designs from books and transfer them to your quilt top before sandwiching the layers together.

You can also purchase quilting stencils. These designs should be traced onto the quilt top before sandwiching the layers together. Usually chalk, a water-soluble marker or pencil that can be erased is used for this process. Please check to make sure that the marker you plan to use will wash out.

Stencil design choices are limitless. They may be purchased, or you can design and make your own.

### Professional Longarm Quilting

If you love piecing quilts but not the quilting process, you can pay a longarm quilter to quilt for you. Talk to other quilters about longarm quilters in your area to get recommendations. Ask to look at samples of workmanship from a few different longarm quilters. Just like any other talent, some people are better at this than others.

Your quilter will probably show you many quilting designs from which to choose. Many professional longarm quilters are capable of creating original designs that will make your quilt one of a kind. Of course, the more quilting that is done, the more expensive the cost for quilting will be.

For longarm quilting, you will need to provide backing fabric and batting that is a good 4"–6" larger than the size of the quilt top all the way around. This extra fabric is needed to attach the quilt to the frame.

Do not layer your quilt top, batting and backing into a quilt "sandwich." Instead, take the separate layers to the longarm quilter, and he or she will do the rest.

## The Quilt Backing

### Purchasing Backing Fabric

Measure your finished quilt top vertically and horizontally, and add 4" for each side (that will add 8" to each measurement) for the size needed for your backing piece. This allows for some shifting during the quilting process.

For example, if your quilt top finishes at 54" x 78", you will need a minimum of 62" x 86" backing fabric. *Note: Batting should be cut to the same size as the backing piece.*

## Preparing the Backing

It is possible to buy 108"–118"-wide backing fabric. Although you don't have as many choices in fabric selection, this option eliminates the need to join 42"-wide fabric pieces together to get the needed size. This option is actually less expensive than buying regular 44"–45"-wide yardage, but this fabric also has a different thread count. This could cause a bit of uneven shrinkage. If all the fabric in your quilt has been washed prior to being used in the quilt, then the backing should be washed before being added to the back of the quilt.

For the Twist & Turn Quilt, you need to purchase yardage in the length needed, which is 86". For the example above, 5 yards would be enough.

If using 42"-usable-width fabric, you will have a wide selection of fabric choices. For the example above, you will need to buy twice the length of the quilt to have enough fabric, which would be 5 yards of 42"-usable-width fabric. This yardage would be cut into two equal pieces and seamed together to result in an 84" x 86" backing, which would need to be trimmed to 62" x 86". *Note: Before seaming the two lengths together, remove the selvage edges along the sides to be joined.*

The last option is to piece the back with your left-over scraps from the project. This can be a lot of fun, but will take longer. The up side to this is you can make a two-sided quilt, expanding your creativity.

I have used all three choices at one time or another for my quilts. It really depends on my vision for the quilt. By the time I am ready to quilt, I have a clear-cut idea of what it needs and what I want it to be. Again, this is a personal choice. It is best to wait until you have finished the quilt top to purchase the backing. You never know what you may decide and buying prematurely could cost you double.

## Preparing the Quilt

### Sandwiching the Layers

Sandwiching the batting between the completed quilt top and the prepared backing is the next step.

If you will be hand-quilting, you will probably use a frame. If you are using a floor frame, you will not need to pin or baste the layers together. The layers will be flat after mounting on the frame. If using a small lap or free-standing frame, basting is the best option because the pins might get in the way when moving the frame from place to place.

If you will be quilting using your sewing machine, the layers need to be sandwiched, and then pinned or basted together to be held flat and prevent shifting during quilting.

The easiest way to sandwich a bed-size quilt is to do it on a floor. Carpeted floors work best. There are a few different ways to do this. One way is to press and lay the backing fabric right side down on the floor or carpet. Either tape the backing to the floor/carpet or pin with T-pins. Either method works well.

Next, center the batting over the backing fabric and smooth out all the wrinkles. If you have purchased packaged batting, place it in a dryer on low to fluff it and get rid of the folds prior to use.

Lay the quilt top right side up on top of the batting. Smooth out all the seams and be sure not to distort the shape. Once you are satisfied with the layering, start in the center of the quilt and place quilter's curved safety pins about 6" apart in all directions. Pin all the way to the edges.

If you are planning to stitch-in-the-ditch, try not to pin too closely to the seams. If you do, you will find yourself moving pins while trying to quilt.

### Basting Spray vs. Pinning

I do not normally recommend basting spray, but that is a personal choice. Basting spray is hard to work with for large projects. It is hard to smooth out when it wants to stick. It does however, work quite well for small projects that do not take a lot of smoothing.

### Hand Basting

The other option is hand basting with thread to hold your sandwiched bundle together.

To do this, use all-purpose thread and make long running stitches back and forth at 6" intervals. It works the same as the pinning, but takes much more time. The basting stitches should be removed after quilting is complete. If quilting stitches are on top of basting stitches, the basting is sometimes hard to remove.

## Quilting

You have decided on the quilting method, and you have chosen a quilting design and marked it on the quilt top. Now that the quilt layers are sandwiched, and pinned or basted, you are ready to quilt.

Like basting or pinning, it is best to begin in the center and work toward the outer edges. You may remove the pins as you go, but the hand-basting will stay in until the quilting is completed. Quilt on the marked lines or in any other desired pattern until the quilting is completed.

### Hand Quilting
Hand quilting is the traditional way to quilt. It is done with a good sharp between needle and quilting thread, usually on a frame. If you have lots of time, and you enjoy handwork, you might enjoy hand quilting. There is nothing like the satisfaction of finishing a hand-quilted piece.

### Quilting With Your Sewing Machine
You may use your sewing machine to quilt your sandwiched quilt. Different methods/patterns are described in the Hand or Sewing-Machine section starting on page 29.

This method is not for everyone. It requires lots of practice and a good relationship with your sewing machine.

It is best to start learning to quilt on your sewing machine on a small project and work your way up to a bed-size quilt.

## Binding
Once the quilting is complete, remove any remaining pins and/or basting. Trim the excess batting and backing even with the edges of the quilt top, making sure the quilt remains square. Use your outer border seam as a guide to trim the excess batting and backing. It should give you an easy and fairly accurate measurement. The quilt is now ready for an edge finish or binding.

There are several ways to add bindings, and then again, some quilters finish their quilts without bindings. My personal preference is to bind my quilts—for me, it is part of the design element. Binding is the final touch to the perfect quilt.

The most common binding is a double-folded 2½"-wide strip. Once you are comfortable with the how-tos, then you can explore different ways, sizes and methods for binding. I like to use a 2"-wide strip—I find that I like a tight binding with no "empty" space on the outer edge of the binding. I am very fussy about the binding edges aligning from the front to the back. To begin, join the cut

binding strips on the short ends with diagonal seams to make a long strip; trim seams and press open. Fold the strip in half with wrong sides together along the length to make a double-layered strip.

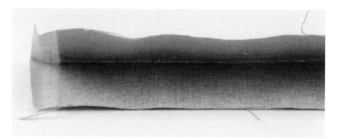

Before applying the binding to your quilt, unfold the strip on one end and fold about a 3" section over in a 45-degree angle with wrong sides together.

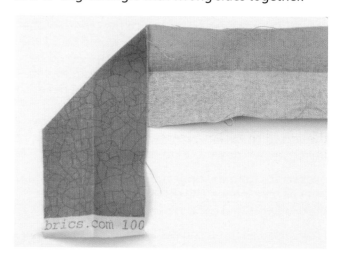

Then fold top down, folding the end of your binding strip so that you create a pocket.

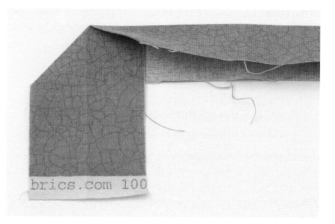

Starting in the middle of a side of your trimmed and squared quilt sandwich, place the binding strip end with the folded pocket, on the right side of the quilt and with raw edges together.

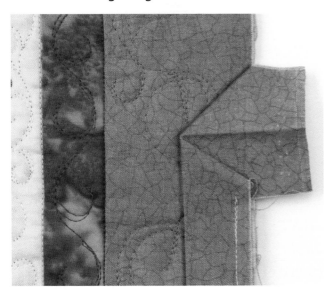

Using a ¼" seam allowance, sew along the remaining distance of the side, stopping ¼" from the corner and pivot and make a 45-degree seam to the corner as shown in Figure 1.

**Figure 1**

Fold the binding strip over and up creating another 45-degree angle as shown in Figure 2. Fold end down and line up with the side. Starting at the top, stitch down the side and repeat the same process at each corner.

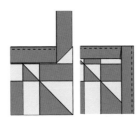

**Figure 2**

When you reach the side you started on, stop about 2" before you reach the folded pocket. Line up and pin into place, trim the binding strip at a 45-degree angle so that it will fit into the pocket.

Finish sewing the seam in place.

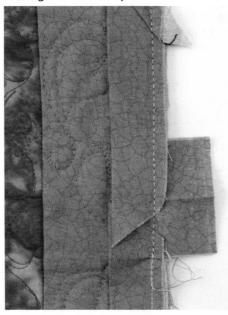

### Tips & Techniques

• *As you are sewing the binding to your quilt, stop 3" before you get to a corner and mark a dot ¼" in from both directions to make a pivot point for a 45-degree angle at the corner. Don't mark before you have gotten close to the corner. Don't mark it before you have gotten close to the corner.*

Trim the tab even with the edge of the quilt.

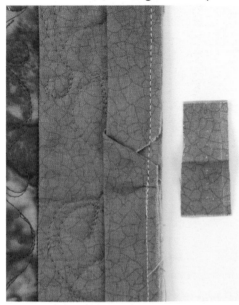

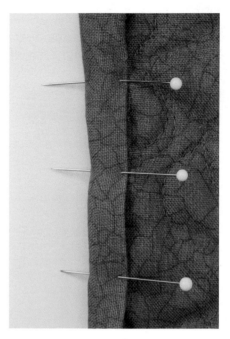

You are now ready to sew your binding down by hand or machine. *Note: I prefer stitching by hand. It has a much neater look, and as a beginner I would suggest you do your binding this way.* Machine-stitching a binding in place takes a lot of practice.

Begin by slipstitching the front diagonal where the binding ends join.

Instead of using pins on the binding, you may want to use binding clips.

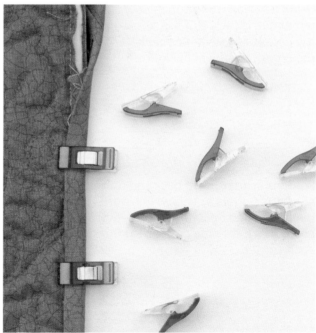

Turn the binding to the back side of the quilt and slipstitch edges in place to cover the raw edge and seam line.

Start stitching where you began putting on the binding by machine and when you get to the end, tuck the end in the pocket and secure. ❖

# Documenting Your Quilt

When you have finished and are admiring your first quilt, there is one more thing you should do before you use it, hang it or give it away. It's one of the most important steps in the process, but it is also the one that gets overlooked the most—documenting your quilt.

Just know that someday someone will hold your quilt and the question that comes out of their mouth will be, "I wonder who made this quilt?" It may be a granddaughter or great-granddaughter who is looking for a connection to the past. It could be a complete stranger who is looking for a connection to the maker.

Start documenting your quilts today. Make it a tradition you follow with every quilt you make. Leaving a message on your quilt not only helps date it in later years, it also is the perfect personal touch to let the receiver of the quilt know just how important he or she is to you. Whether it is a gift for a wedding, for a new baby or just because, a label with a message will make it all the more special.

We are giving you a label, designed by Brooke Smith from her book, *Quilt Labels for All Occasions*, (available at Clotilde.com). Trace the design onto a piece of solid-color fabric, using a window or a light box, with a water-soluble marker. Then retrace the design outlines and text with a fine-point, permanant fabric marker. You can color in the design to match your colors, add your own message or make it your own.

Trim the label so you have ¼" to turn under on all sides. Press the edges to the wrong side, and place on a corner on the back of the quilt. Hand-stitch the label to the back of the quilt using a slipstitch or a decorative buttonhole stitch. ❖

## Tips & Techniques

• *If you don't keep your first quilt for yourself, at least take a picture of it. A few years from now you will be totally amazed at how far you have come in your quilting.*

• *It is always inspiring to look back to see how many quilts you have made. Keep a binder page with fabric samples and other notes about each quilt. If you have given most of them away, looking through these pages and photos will help you remember your experiences and the satisfaction that comes from making beautiful quilts.*

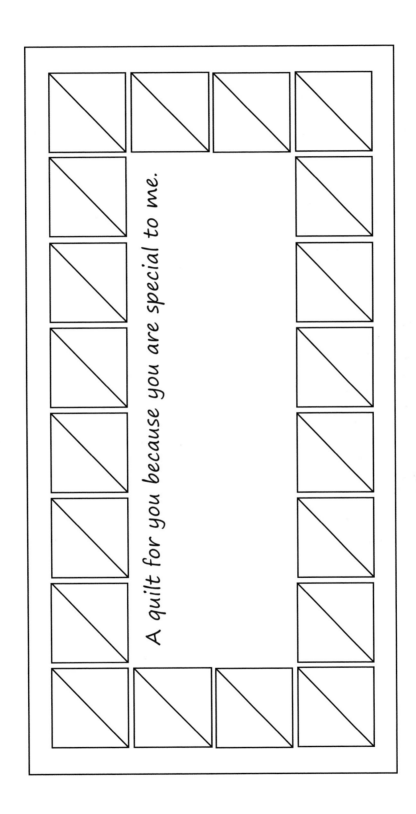

A quilt for you because you are special to me.

House of White Birches, Berne, Indiana 46711   Clotilde.com

# Gallery of Quilts

*This quilt was stitched and quilted by Abby Geha. This is Abby's first quilt. She selected fabrics with a lot of contrast between the light and dark fabrics. She added two new fabrics for her borders and binding, a hot pink inner border to add color and a black solid for the wide border. The hot pink binding frames the quilt nicely.*

*This quilt was stitched and quilted by Carol Listenberger. In order to create this quilt setting Carol stitched half of the blocks as mirror images of the original block. She added a third fabric for the narrow inner border, selecting a color found in her focus fabric. She used her focus fabric for the outer border and binding. Look for the concentric light and dark diamonds in her quilt.*

*This quilt was stitched and quilted by Pamela Pease. Pamela is an experienced quilter, but she learned new and easier ways to do some tasks while making this quilt. The design of her quilt blocks (the setting) really "pops" because of the high contrast of her two fabrics. She used the lighter of her two fabrics for the narrow inner border and the darker fabric for the wide border and binding.*

*This quilt was stitched and quilted by Stephanie Franklin. Stephanie was a true beginner with no previous quilting knowledge. She arranged the blocks so that the body of her quilt has light and dark blocks set on point. She selected a third fabric for the narrow inner border to emphasize her design.*

*This quilt was stitched and quilted by Karlyn Bauman. It is her first quilt. Instead of choosing a light and dark fabric, Karlyn selected two contrasting colors. Karlyn did not add an inner border, using one fabric for the border and the second fabric for the binding.*

# Alternate Settings

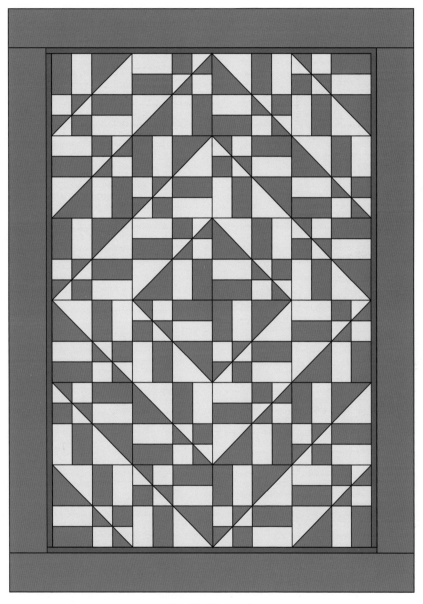

**Double Diamonds**
Alternate Placement Diagram

House of White Birches, Berne, Indiana 46711  Clotilde.com

44

**Twist & Turn**
Alternate Placement Diagram

**Twist & Turn**
Alternate Placement Diagram

**Twist & Turn**
Alternate Placement Diagram

**Twist & Turn**
Alternate Placement Diagram

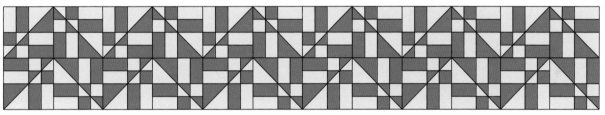

**Twist & Turn**
Alternate Placement Diagram

**Reversed Stripes**
Alternate Placement Diagram

House of White Birches, Berne, Indiana 46711   Clotilde.com

**Reversed Stripes**
Alternate Placement Diagram

**Twist & Turn**
Alternate Placement Diagram

House of White Birches, Berne, Indiana 46711   Clotilde.com

# METRIC CONVERSION CHARTS

## Metric Conversions

| Canada/U.S. Measurement | | Multiplied by | Metric Measurement |
|---|---|---|---|
| yards | x | .9144 | = metres (m) |
| yards | x | 91.44 | = centimetres (cm) |
| inches | x | 2.54 | = centimetres (cm) |
| inches | x | 25.40 | = millimetres (mm) |
| inches | x | .0254 | = metres (m) |

| Canada/U.S. Measurement | | Multiplied by | Metric Measurement |
|---|---|---|---|
| centimetres | x | .3937 | = inches |
| metres | x | 1.0936 | = yards |

## Standard Equivalents

| Canada/U.S. Measurement | | Metric Measurement | | |
|---|---|---|---|---|
| ⅛ inch | = | 3.20 mm | = | 0.32 cm |
| ¼ inch | = | 6.35 mm | = | 0.635 cm |
| ⅜ inch | = | 9.50 mm | = | 0.95 cm |
| ½ inch | = | 12.70 mm | = | 1.27 cm |
| ⅝ inch | = | 15.90 mm | = | 1.59 cm |
| ¾ inch | = | 19.10 mm | = | 1.91 cm |
| ⅞ inch | = | 22.20 mm | = | 2.22 cm |
| 1 inches | = | 25.40 mm | = | 2.54 cm |
| ⅛ yard | = | 11.43 cm | = | 0.11 m |
| ¼ yard | = | 22.86 cm | = | 0.23 m |
| ⅜ yard | = | 34.29 cm | = | 0.34 m |
| ½ yard | = | 45.72 cm | = | 0.46 m |
| ⅝ yard | = | 57.15 cm | = | 0.57 m |
| ¾ yard | = | 68.58 cm | = | 0.69 m |
| ⅞ yard | = | 80.00 cm | = | 0.80 m |
| 1 yard | = | 91.44 cm | = | 0.91 m |
| 1⅛ yards | = | 102.87 cm | = | 1.03 m |
| 1¼ yards | = | 114.30 cm | = | 1.14 m |

| Canada/U.S. Measurement | | | | Metric Measurement |
|---|---|---|---|---|
| 1⅜ yards | = | 125.73 cm | = | 1.26 m |
| 1½ yards | = | 137.16 cm | = | 1.37 m |
| 1⅝ yards | = | 148.59 cm | = | 1.49 m |
| 1¾ yards | = | 160.02 cm | = | 1.60 m |
| 1⅞ yards | = | 171.44 cm | = | 1.71 m |
| 2 yards | = | 182.88 cm | = | 1.83 m |
| 2⅛ yards | = | 194.31 cm | = | 1.94 m |
| 2¼ yards | = | 205.74 cm | = | 2.06 m |
| 2⅜ yards | = | 217.17 cm | = | 2.17 m |
| 2½ yards | = | 228.60 cm | = | 2.29 m |
| 2⅝ yards | = | 240.03 cm | = | 2.40 m |
| 2¾ yards | = | 251.46 cm | = | 2.51 m |
| 2⅞ yards | = | 262.88 cm | = | 2.63 m |
| 3 yards | = | 274.32 cm | = | 2.74 m |
| 3⅛ yards | = | 285.75 cm | = | 2.86 m |
| 3¼ yards | = | 297.18 cm | = | 2.97 m |
| 3⅜ yards | = | 308.61 cm | = | 3.09 m |
| 3½ yards | = | 320.04 cm | = | 3.20 m |
| 3⅝ yards | = | 331.47 cm | = | 3.31 m |
| 3¾ yards | = | 342.90 cm | = | 3.43 m |
| 3⅞ yards | = | 354.32 cm | = | 3.54 m |
| 4 yards | = | 365.76 cm | = | 3.66 m |
| 4⅛ yards | = | 377.19 cm | = | 3.77 m |
| 4¼ yards | = | 388.62 cm | = | 3.89 m |
| 4⅜ yards | = | 400.05 cm | = | 4.00 m |
| 4½ yards | = | 411.48 cm | = | 4.11 m |
| 4⅝ yards | = | 422.91 cm | = | 4.23 m |
| 4¾ yards | = | 434.34 cm | = | 4.34 m |
| 4⅞ yards | = | 445.76 cm | = | 4.46 m |
| 5 yards | = | 457.20 cm | = | 4.57 m |

HOUSE of
WHITE
BIRCHES
PUBLISHERS
SINCE 1947

**Learn to Make a Quilt From Start to Finish** is published by DRG, 306 East Parr Road, Berne, IN 46711. Printed in USA. Copyright © 2011 DRG. All rights reserved. This publication may not be reproduced in part or in whole without written permission from the publisher.

**RETAIL STORES:** If you would like to carry this pattern book or any other DRG publications, visit DRGwholesale.com

Every effort has been made to ensure that the instructions in this pattern book are complete and accurate. We cannot, however, take responsibility for human error, typographical mistakes or variations in individual work. Please visit ClotildeCustomerCare.com to check for pattern updates.

ISBN: 978-1-59217-326-6

1 2 3 4 5 6 7 8 9